MAY IT BE

Growing a Genuine Life

First published by The From a Friend Project, March 2017

Cover design by Hannah P. Mode
Book design by Adam Robinson
for Good Book Developers

Printed in the United States of America

For more information, please visit
www.ChrissaVentrelle.com

MAY IT BE

Growing a Genuine Life

Chrissa Ventrelle

To Drew, Brooke, and Ryan
May it be for you.

CONTENTS

WAYFINDING

May you slow down to notice
that what appears singular
is often part of something grander,
just as a stand of quaking aspen
looks to be a grove of individual trees
until a bit of digging
reveals a single massive organism
that sends sprouts upwards
from its widespread web of roots.

May you see yourself
in the ancient arched sequoia
that bridges the brook,
in the lichen that covers its underbelly,
in the termite that harvests its bark,
in the hawk perched above,
and the monarch fluttering past.
May all of nature be your looking glass.

May you listen for the call
of who you are
and stand tall
in the posture
of that self-assurance—
sure-footed,
steady-handed,
calm-minded,
drawn ever nearer
to your true vocation.

May you get there.
Whether you sprint
or side wind
or skip
or stagger,
may you get there.
And then there.
And then there.

Though the pace may not be quick,
nor the path straight,
nor the directions exact,
may you heed the call.
Go any way.

May you trust in yourself
both today and tomorrow,
as the fawn knows that one day
it will run with its mother's agility,
and the cub presumes
it will match its father's strength
in time.

May you cherish your young self
and have faith in your evolution.
May you own your many fleeting iterations
and value the purpose of each phase.

May you be you.
May you grasp the sacredness
of your singularity
in mind,
in perspective,
in voice,
in inspiration.

May you embrace your uniqueness,
knowing it is by design.
When self-doubt drains
and confidence wanes,
may you pause
and honor all you are.

May you listen
to the stirrings of your soul—
that flicker of energy,
that jingling vibration,
that unrequited longing.

May you see these visceral urgings
as ushers to your authentic passions.
May you gather up the resolve
to greet these guides
and move ever closer to their source.

May you own the beauty of
your heart,
your mind,
your body.

May you appreciate your grace and gifts,
owning them with quiet confidence,
never dimming your radiance
to match the luminance of others.

May you try, try, try to be gentle with your soul,
emboldening it to shine its most brilliant light.

May you find your element
and make it yours,
just as a bird knows the sky is to fly,
and a fish trusts the sea is to swim.

May you keep watch for
environments that inspire,
experiences where time escapes,
and emotions with the audacity
to feel both complex and sparse.

May you believe
in yourself,
in a higher power,
in others,
in what's possible.

May you marvel
at each living creature
as grace in action
and celebrate
how life strings together
wonder after wonder.

And when miracles line your path,
as they will,
may you embrace them with
gratitude and awe.

WALKING
TOGETHER

May you love and be loved,
embracing its many forms.
May you know boundless, roomy love,
layered in moments both tiny and grand,
leaving your capacious heart
all the bigger
to love and love more.

May you cherish friends
who value friendship
as deeply as you do,
who yearn to see all of you,
who prod you to grow,
who bring joy to the doldrums,
who forgive moments gone awry.

May you hold close the friends
who elevate the title
to a sacred state,
a place of grace and mercy,
where apprehensions are lifted,
and trust is cemented.

May you treasure these friends,
for they are sprinkled sparingly
through our lives,
like turquoise sea glass
on a beige beach.

May you love a child.
May you sense the sincerity
of a small-armed embrace,
the recklessness of a wild temper tantrum,
the expression of generosity
created by awkward hands.

May you harness the stamina
to answer a whirlwind of whys,
the patience to assuage a steady flow of worries,
the spontaneity to stretch a spot of fun,
and the humility to nurture
a young heart to fullness.

May you stitch generations together
with stories from then and now,
weaving love from young to old.

May you lean in to hear
the elders share their
patchwork tales
of youthful shenanigans,
of wisdom well-earned,
of love lost and found,
and failures that preceded
success.

May you trace the threads of legacy
and celebrate the colorful cloth of kinship.

May you keep your circle of friends
broad and expansive,
holding space for new relationships
that invigorate and challenge.

May you plant yourself in situations
where fresh people and ideas
prompt your heart to flutter anew.

And when you meet a stranger
who appears to offer little,
may you still welcome the encounter,
honoring every person as a teacher.

May you choose a mate
with the integrity of an oak,
one who
grows deep roots,
adapts to the terrain,
withstands storms,
produces vibrant colors,
regenerates season after season,
and offers shelter and shade.

May you find a champion—
a mentor who asks, "*How bright will you shine?*"
a guide who leads to the loftier place,
a teacher who offers critique and discernment.

May you rise in their wisdom,
wax gracefully under their care,
and extend this gift to another.

May you hold close
the depth and breadth
of parental love
and the dedication
of this sacred role.

May this devotion
make life thrive,
like carbon,
bonding to build
something greater—
from a hard diamond,
disperser of light,
to gritty charcoal,
bringer of heat.

May you rest in this pure love,
and its many forms,
all anchored in unconditionality.

May you be blessed
with a friendship that endures
beyond the parameters of natural phases
and evolves over decades,
perhaps a generation or more.

May you experience a friendship
built on countless touchpoints
layered one over the other—
a source of renewal
season after season
that intertwines a history
shared between two hearts,
leaving lasting markings
of genuine connection.

May you seek out kindred spirits
bound together by a thirst to thrive.

May you watch in wonder
as individuals
sprout into community,
a patient process of braiding
separate vines
into one.

May you serve this group
as both the stable base
of the strong root stalk
and the young scion
grafted on it.

May you discover utility
in both roles,
as it takes both
stalk and scion
to bear new fruit.

SMOOTHING THE TRAIL FOR OTHERS

May you litter your path
with seeds of kindness,
spurring wildflowers
to bloom in your wake.

May others do the same,
so you feel the brave rhythm
of receiving from those ahead
and leaving for those behind.

And like those flowers,
may you grow.

May you consider this recipe
for deep satisfaction—
hustle till needs are met,
till your cup is full
plus a little more,
then pause,
befriending the space
between need and want.

May you use this room
to give freely,
to fold in good works,
to taste the richness of gratitude,
and to savor the joy of enough.

May you turn towards
the world's most pressing problems,
serving as a harbinger of hope
to the forgotten places
where scarcity rules and despair reigns.

May you illuminate the darkest alleys
and make smooth the path
of those saddled with the heaviest load.

May you cradle another in their suffering
even when all you can offer is witness to it,
for even a thin blanket insulates on a frosty night,
and a small shade patch
protects from scalding heat.

May you experience the blessing
of walking with another
as they step towards healing,
as simple solidarity can bring solace,
allowing a soothing peace to spread.

May you say yes to the barn raising
for the neighbor in need,
as you need not the skills of
a master builder to contribute.

May you lend your most valuable tools—
a willing spirit and
confidence in the community.

May you bring restoration
to both the barn
and those it shelters.

May you give your whole presence
when you listen to another,
as the impact of feeling truly heard
can nearly match the power of love.

May you see the value of this gift,
perhaps of greater worth
than even inspired advice.

May you be a song
with a melody that anchors,
a harmony that inspires,
and a refrain that nurtures.

May your music offer solace
and serve as a gift to others.
May it ring true to the life that is yours,
and may you boldly sing it.

May you serve others
with an active hope,
relying on it as a balm for pain
and an antidote for paralysis
in the face of challenge.

And when you feel
the tug of injustice or
the pull of suffering,
may you marry
hope and action
to catalyze change.

TRAIL
MARKERS

May you be like spiders' silk:
strong yet stretchable,
durable yet flexible,
a marvel of form and function—
a home, a net, a catcher of dew—
may your web be all this too.

May you simplify,
paring down
to what you love
and what you use,
creating space for clarity
and room for ideas
to germinate.

May you weed out clutter
and cultivate calm,
shaping where you live
into a place
that rejuvenates and inspires.

May you honor the small,
for tiny tinder, not hefty logs, spark a fire.
May you celebrate the overlooked,
for a mighty river trickles first
from a hillside rill,
a solitary candle can illuminate a cavern,
a single seed can birth bushels of apples,
and one smile can ignite a love story.

May you know the comfort of home.
May you feel safe in its ebbs and flows,
its high and low tides,
its sunrises and sunsets.

May you sense the nuances of your sanctuary—
the hour by the orange streaks across the ridge,
the month by the sweetness of plums
on the unkempt tree,
the season by the return of mourning doves.
May you love your place and relax in its shelter.

May you treasure silence,
holding it as a rare gift
with the power to nourish.

May you use stillness as a tonic
to shrink a problem
from boulder to pebble
or multiply a fraction of a thought
into infinite possibilities.

May you push beyond
the vulnerability that leeches on quiet
and sit with both the uncertainty
and aspirations it exposes.

And in this tranquility,
may your spirit be restored.

May you bake bread
to untangle days knotted with anxiety
and crippled by disappointment.

May you watch flour, water, and yeast
meld into nourishment.
May you work the dough
with the heels of your hands,
then rest while it does too,
noting how you both grow
malleable after a break.

In darkness, in suffering, in chaos,
may you hold fast to the staff of life
and be assured you will rise again.

May you read
every day
in the cracks
or in wide expanses,
making friends with
characters who encourage,
ideas that inspire,
concepts that challenge,
and emotions that foster empathy.

May you read
for your heart,
for your mind,
for your soul,
to calm nerves,
to master a task,
to laugh,
to connect,
to marvel at the vastness of the world,
to grasp the truth of the past,
to float into the possibilities of the future.

May you learn about yourself
page by page.

May you befriend time
and see it as an asset,
not an enemy to beat,
nor a vessel to fill,
nor a debt to pay.

May you appreciate that some days
sit dense as blackberry bramble
in late summer,
while others hang bare like a sycamore
standing skeletal in winter.

May you craft your seasons
with ample space
for breath,
for work,
for love,
for service,
for health,
for play,
and for your spirit to stretch
between each gibbous moon.

May you sleep
a slumber of safety—
so sound,
so deep,
so soft.

May you welcome rest
and greet renewal.

When the time comes
to close a chapter,
may you honor the ending
as much as the beginning,
just as a hug is an act of
both claiming and releasing.
May you go with integrity,
finish with dignity.

IN THE BACK COUNTRY

May you allow yourself
the space,
the grace,
and the sense of place
to take "wrong" turns.

May you be brave enough
to let your path be crooked,
disfigured by naughty adventures
and knotted with bumps
born from the shrink and stretch
of what's beneath.

Though tidy paved roads
and promptness
have their purpose,
may you not always take
the measured route.

May you veer off
from time to time
and see what evolves.
And in pursuit of the unexplored,
may you travel the road meant for you.

May you make peace with the unscripted,
recalling how a rogue storm can deliver ships
to unknown ports,
an untuned piano can create a new sound,
and vile mold can morph into medicine.

May you expect the arrival of
the unscheduled and unpredicted,
and fold them into your plans.

May you celebrate
the risks you take
regardless of the outcome.

May you reach so fully
that you propel forward
even when the headwinds
of rejection
and the gravity of failure
offer worthy resistance.

May you persist,
trusting the act of deep stretching
will leave you taller.

May you admire the creations
of a distant place,
made by hands that may not resemble yours
but whose fingers grip the brush as yours do
and whose palms warm clay just the same.

May you admire the call
to shape and to share,
from hand to hand,
from home to home.

May you explore ideas that feel foreign,
born from a mind with a different approach,
but whose thoughts ricochet as yours do
and whose emotions vibrate just the same.

May you embrace the opportunity
to express and debate,
from mind to mind,
from life to life.

May you befriend the faraway—
its people and its cultures—
and draw it near.

May you aim to expand your *joie de vivre* and carry a few hobbies in your quiver—interests that stretch, delight, and renew, pursuits that attract a variety of people, and activities that relax or exhilarate.

May you dare to look where
the dimpled melon drips with juicy pulp,
the bland geode conceals sparkling crystal,
and the unassuming book reveals stunning prose.

May you search
for treasure hiding in plain sight,
for sustenance in the unlikely,
and for beauty in the ordinary.

May you feed your hunger
for fresh ideas
and quench your thirst
for understanding.

May you refrain from
growing insecure
when new teachings
overwhelm you,
and choose instead
to invite a concept
to warm slowly
in your mind,
as if dough rising,
until it grows
soft and pliant
and yours to shape.

May you rely on your intuition
to determine
who is worthy to enter
your sanctum of trust.

May you lean into your intuition
to wisely discern
which course will fracture
and which will repair.

And may you heed your intuition
when it barks loudly,
remembering we are first animals
with ancient instincts to survive.

May you show compassion for your imperfections
and observe your flaws with detachment,
carefully choosing which to accept and which to fix.

May you notice a bruised fruit
still tastes sweet,
a creaky door still opens wide,
and a bended tree still offers shade.

May you understand
that blemishes mark us all,
but the joyful and wise
transform these reservoirs of shame
into endearing wellsprings of humor.

AT THE
TREE LINE

May you flourish
like edelweiss,
the sweet flower
dressed in delicate white,
which thrives where even
sturdy pines wither
amidst thin air
and harsh weather.

May you learn
to bloom
in rocky limestone,
inspiring song
and embodying
rugged beauty.

May your words be a lantern,
guiding others through darkness
to a sanctuary bathed in light.

May your ideas be a torch,
heating the conversation
and sparking new debate.

May your actions be a bonfire,
inspiring many to gather round
and warm themselves with story and song.

May your wit be the dancing flame
that brightens shadows with humor
and marries the blues with yellow laughter.

May you ask the big questions,
the kind that break you open—
What type of person do I want to be?
What do I believe?
What will I leave behind?

May you feel the sting of these inquiries,
sometimes exhausting in their weight,
but may you hold them anyway,
for wisdom rarely comes in a torrent,
but more often in a soothing mist.

May you return here again and again
to widen, to deepen, and to observe,
while trusting clarity will emerge,
if only drop by drop.

May you speak the simple words,
the ones you think needn't be said
or the ones you'd rather not say.
May you let these be heard—
please,
thank you,
I'm sorry,
well done,
I love you,
and the hardest of all,
I forgive you.
May you risk saying too much
rather than too little.

May you recognize that strokes of genius
are more fiction than fact,
as most brilliant ideas
are born from countless revisions
of an original fuzzy notion,
first hidden among shadows and haze.

May you dare to foster an idea
from opaque to translucent to sheer,
increasing its clarity
until finally light shines through,
making its radiance visible to all.

May you summon the courage
to speak the words
that convey your deepest stirrings—
words that mirror your values,
words that signal appreciation,
words that evoke passion,
and words with the weight
to convey sadness
and outrage
and frustration.

May you speak with the conviction of one
who knows what must be said,
and then may you hear, hear, hear
the language of another.

May you talk to Spirit
throughout the day
in a flowing dialogue
that moves freely,
from the placid waters of a whisper
to the choppy swell of a rant
to the swirling eddy of a laugh,
but always bearing truth
in its undercurrent.

May you be assured you are heard
even if the tides don't change as you desire.
Listen carefully for the wash of Wisdom's voice,
a faithful companion in open waters.

May you build a spiritual nest,
a place to rest,
to inspire,
and to nurture.

May you gather twigs of tenderness
and layer sticks for support
while leaving space for others to do the same.

As you grow in this refuge,
may you feel the sacredness of solidarity,
the courage born from close community,
and the faith to fly.

May you examine your faith,
study its beliefs, its origins,
its history, and its future.

As with a pinecone,
may you look at
the tree from which this faith grew,
finger the curves
that form its scales,
and observe the
many creatures it nourishes.

Once you know it well,
by heart and by mind,
may you ask if its offerings
will sustain you too.

May you seek wisdom
as you wade through
the shallow waters
of the religious doctrine
taught in your youth
and into the deep pools
of adult faith.

VISTAS

May you climb to higher ground
where vistas inspire
and expanses invite.

May you scramble
over impulses
to resist,
to complain,
to waste,
to stay in the muck,
and elevate yourself
to where growth grows,
movements move,
and thoughts expand.

May you explore
what's next,
what's just,
what's true.

May you find happiness
in the climb
and beckon others to trek
out of small days
and into a grander realm.

May you seek perspective,
pausing from time to time
to observe your story from on high,
marveling at the distance covered
step by step by step.

May you view the vastness
of your voyage—
the sunshine and storms,
the kyles and open waters,
the humid and arid lands.

May you honor what's behind you—
learnings amassed,
mistakes discarded,
people shaped by knowing you.

And then go on.

May you examine
the loose threads of your life
and pause before pulling,
knowing an impulsive tug
can unravel stitches of labor and love.

May you seek first
to repair,
to mend,
to hem
with compassion.
May you be a seamstress of restoration,
a tailor of reconciliation.

May you stand tall
when the urge is to cower.

May you shine
when your light feels dim.

May you speak loudly
when critics hope you'll whisper.

May you blossom
when defamers expect you'll wither.

May you resist the inclinations
to hide,
to shrink,
to slump.

May you rise.

May your life be a harvest,
abundant in adventures
and rich in relationships.

May you feast
on what your hands and heart
have lovingly cultivated over seasons,
while still preserving some
for darker times.

As you till your days like soil
and a legacy grows,
may you also taste
what sprouts wildly
from the earth.

May you be farmer and forager,
nurturer of the familiar
and seeker of the unexplored.

May you fix your vision
on the big picture,
pausing often to note
if the cadence of your days
matches the rhythm
of your higher callings.

May your actions
in the ordinary
mirror what you value
in the whole,
so the minor moments amass
into something more.

May you shed old fears that no longer fit,
the worries from childhood
now tattered and frayed,
the anxious habits of yesterday
so ill-suited for today.

May you discard these distresses,
so dated and dusty,
and free that space
for lightness
and brightness
and joy.

May you experience the world
as a child does—
full-bodied and full-hearted.

May you stand in awe of all,
the greatness and the grandeur,
yet see the sacred in the small.

May you touch and taste
both the ripe and the raw,
with gratitude for both.

And may you wonder.

VALLEYS

May you experience rebirth
in the wake of ruin,
just as the whitebark pine
relies on the searing flames
of a forest fire
to open its cones and
release its seeds,
freeing what was once locked away
to grow tender new shoots.

May you be kind to yourself
as the pain of loss or betrayal
heaves and hits upon you.

May you find a salve that soothes—
the restoring hum of nature,
the attentive ear of a friend,
the prayer offered upwards.

May you uncover strength
in the struggle,
resisting the urge to stay
in the clammy dark too long.

May you do as the daffodil
and push skyward from bulb
through rocky soil,
knowing light and warmth beckon
on the other side of blackness.

May you sit with struggle and suffering,
unwelcome guests that they are.

Though you may resent their coming
without invitation
and stew about their disruptive stay,
may you be assured
the day will come—
even if a long, long time from now—
when you will understand,
or at least accept,
the purpose of their visit.

May you one day notice
these intruders left a gift,
a payment for your troubles,
in the form of
empathy,
gratitude,
fortitude,
or wisdom.

May you make good use of it
when these visitors knock again.

When structures around you crumble to ruins,
may you rebuild atop the rubble,
starting first with columns of character,
then securing each new stone with integrity,
the foundation for all else to rest.

May you unravel your doubts
like a ball of mangy yarn
abandoned in a weathered sewing basket.

May you unwind these insecurities inch by inch,
exposing fibers of fear to fresh air,
releasing what is tightly wound into fluid form.

May this yarn grow useful once free to move,
if only as a bow on a package
or a string on a child's kite.

May you address a problem
in its morning
when the water lies still
and early light is soft—
before waves curve wildly,
swells break unpredictably,
and the wind blows harshly.

But when you are caught
in an afternoon monsoon,
may you use
the strong, still voice of your core
as a rudder to steer you home.

May you tend to your fire,
feed it,
keep it aflame
in a dancing blaze
of gold and indigo
that roars and snaps with heat.

But when that hearth
offers barely a whisper of warmth,
may you simply keep the embers alive—
even when your energy slumps low,
even when darkness beckons louder,
even when no guests will knock.

For it is easier to revive a small spark
than to start again from tinder and match.

May you call for help in dark times,
no matter if it's dusk
or dawn
or midnight.

May your plea be answered
with attentive ears,
calming words,
and wisdom.

May you unlock what shackles your dream
by exploring the difference
between a legitimate reservation
and the creation of an insecure mind.

May you shed the immaterial and destructive,
grow comfortable with uncertainty,
and push forward with a ferocity
that surprises even you.

May you regard hope as a choice
and be infectious in that.

May you believe in believing
and center around expectancy.

May you return to hope
when no stars twinkle in the night sky
or the sun burns too bright.

May you hold to hope as a handrail,
a guide from dark to light.

PEAKS

May you relish joy
and radiate with elation
when good news
comes your way.

When delight pays a visit,
may you embrace it,
hold its warmth close,
then allow it to build
to its own crescendo.

May you ditch the to do list
and complete this scavenger hunt:
body embraced,
lips kissed,
belly swelled with laughter,
chest puffed with pride,
cheeks tired from smiling,
heart fluttered with anticipation,
soul invigorated by conversation,
muscles loosened from play,
mind soothed by meditation,
stomach satiated by real food.

Along the way
may you discover
peace and passion
in the vast expanses
and nooks and crannies
of your adventures.

May your heart be
deep and wide enough
to genuinely celebrate
the blessings received by others.

May you play,
smile till your cheeks hurt,
laugh till your stomach muscles protest,
and dance till your feet ache.

May you savor the good moments
and sit with your successes,
allowing yourself to soak
in celebration.

May you give thanks for the journey
that landed you here,
for the devotion and dedication
that propelled you onward,
and for the internal belief
that it could be done.

May you put some *zippity* in your *do da*
and simply have fun,
shaking away heavy in favor of light
and trading sadness for joy and delight.

May you laugh hard and giggle often,
letting the occasional snort escape—
a surefire way to shorten the distance
between you and another.

May you receive graciously.

May generosity flow to you,
and may kindness create pathways
that beckon and sustain you.

May love find you
and flourish
in your safekeeping.

May you laugh all the days of your life.

May it be.

ACKNOWLEDGEMENTS

FOR LOVING
DAN VENTRELLE

FOR ENCOURAGING
CAROLYN & ED HARLEY
GINNA GIRZADAS
LAURA ANDES

Dawn Brightbill
Cathy Cooley
Cindy Dougherty
Kaylee Durow
Rachel George
Peter Honigsberg
Susan Lucas
Lissa Resnick
Shirley Savatgy
Shannon Stabler
Anne Stricherz
Daniele Upp
Jennifer Ventrelle

FOR INSPIRING

DREW, BROOKE, and RYAN
VENTRELLE
Grace, Luke, Eve, Allie, Alex,
Kaylan, and Colben

FOR EDITING, DESIGNING, AND PUBLISHING

Tammy Gaylord
Cynthia Leslie-Bole
Christy Mack
Hannah P. Mode
Adam Robinson

Index of First Lines

As a writer and nonprofit executive, Chrissa Harley Ventrelle has written about topics as diverse as international affairs, philanthropic initiatives, and the San Francisco Bay Area's best bakeries. She received a Bachelor of Arts from the University of Notre Dame and a Master of Public Policy from the University of Michigan. Chrissa lives outside San Francisco with her husband and three kids.

May It Be started as a collection of offerings that Chrissa wrote for her oldest son as he graduated from high school and started college. Her hope is that anyone in a time of change will find a blessing on these pages that resonates with where they are now, or where they hope to be.